Behind the Scenes with Coders

SOFTWARE ARCHITECT

Christine Honders

PowerKiDS press.

New York

Published in 2018 by The Rosen Publishing Group, Inc.
29 East 21st Street, New York, NY 10010

First Edition

Editor: Melissa Raé Shofner
Book Design: Mickey Harmon
Interior Layout: Rachel Rising

Photo Credits: Cover, pp. 1, 3–32 (background) Lukas RS/Shutterstock.com; Cover Ariwasabi/Shutterstock.com; Cover whiteMocca/Shutterstock.com; p. 4 Julia Tim/Shutterstock.com; p. 5 https://commons.wikimedia.org/wiki/File:Gottfried_Wilhelm_Leibniz,_Bernhard_Christoph_Francke.jpg; p. 7 ProStockStudio/Shutterstock.com; p. 8 Creative 1/Shutterstock.com; p. 9 Rawpixel.com/Shutterstock.com; p. 11 g-stockstudio/Shutterstock.com; p. 13 ronstik/Shutterstock.com; p. 15 ymgerman/Shutterstock.com; p. 17 RoSonic/Shutterstock.com; p. 19 Vintage Tone/Shutterstock.com; p. 20 Billion Photos/Shutterstock.com; p. 21 Dragon Images/Shutterstock.com; p. 23 Eugene Lazutkin/Moment/Getty Images; p. 25 Cecilie_Arcurs/E+/Getty Images; p. 27 wavebreakmedia/Shutterstock.com; p. 29 Tyler Olson/Shutterstock.com.

Cataloging-in-Publication Data
Names: Honders, Christine.
Title: Software architect / Christine Honders.
Description: New York : PowerKids Press, 2018. | Series: Behind the scenes with coders | Includes index.
Identifiers: ISBN 9781508155751 (pbk.) | ISBN 9781508155690 (library bound) | ISBN 9781508155577 (6 pack)
Subjects: LCSH: Information technology–Vocational guidance–Juvenile literature. | Computer science–Vocational guidance–Juvenile literature.
Classification: LCC T58.5 H66 2018 | DDC 004.023–dc23

Manufactured in the United States of America

CPSIA Compliance Information: Batch ##BS17PK: For Further Information contact Rosen Publishing, New York, New York at 1-800-237-9932

Contents

The World of Coding

Computers are a part of most people's lives today. We use them to do work at school, to shop online, and to keep in touch with our friends. When you visit your favorite website or sit down to play your favorite computer game, do you ever wonder how it all works?

When you go to a website and start clicking around, the computer needs to know what you want to do. Code is a set of instructions and rules that a computer can understand. The people who write these instructions are called coders. Our lives depend on **technology** more and more each day. Coders keep technology advancing to meet our changing needs. One important coding career is that of a **software** architect.

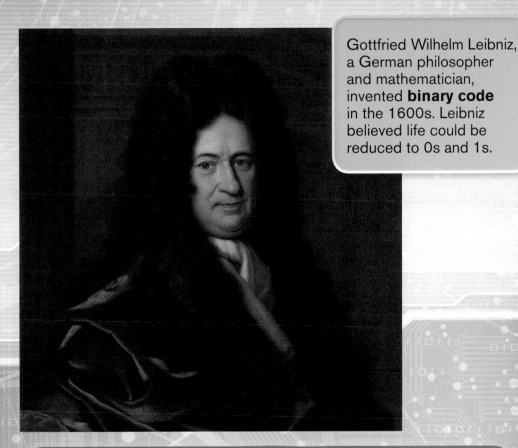

Gottfried Wilhelm Leibniz, a German philosopher and mathematician, invented **binary code** in the 1600s. Leibniz believed life could be reduced to 0s and 1s.

The Importance of Code

Code powers computers, and computers power lots of everyday objects, such as phones, microwaves, and cars. In fact, code powers almost everything that runs on electricity. Computers use binary code, which is difficult for humans to work with because it uses only 0s and 1s. Coders use special coding languages that computers can translate into binary code they understand. There are many different coding languages.

What Is a Software Architect?

Regular architects design and draw plans for new buildings. Software architects (SAs) design and plan software systems. SAs figure out what the software system needs to do and what kind of computer programming and coding would work best. After they create a plan, they stay involved during the whole process to make sure everyone on the team is working toward a common goal. While computer programmers are focused mainly on the software, the SA focuses on the project as a whole.

Software architects must be able to manage a project from its original design to the end result, keeping track of all details in between. Knowing how to code gives them a better understanding of the project and the ability to solve problems on every level.

Software architects keep everyone involved with a project on the same page.

Tech Talk

Some people think that SAs and computer programmers are the same, but their roles are different. Architects design systems and programmers **implement** them. Think of it this way: If they were in a band, the architect would write the music, and the programmers would be the musicians.

A large part of a software architect's job is to listen to what a **client** needs and translate it into **technical** information so programmers can create the perfect software. First, the SA determines what the client wants to accomplish. Then, they decide what kind of technology would work best. During this stage of a project, it's the SA's job to communicate with the client to make sure the software will fit all their needs.

After the project is planned, it's time to develop it. The SA needs to be a leader, provide support to programmers, and keep them focused on the client's needs. SAs are also responsible for testing and **debugging** software and making sure the program is effective and user friendly.

```
1  <!         html>
2  <    >
3  <    >
4      <      charset="utf-8">
5      <    >Javascript 1</  >
6  </    >
7  <    >
8      <    >
9          var str = "Lorem Ipsum"
10         var number = 1;
11         var numberSecond = 2.5;
12         var bool = true;
13         var undef;
14         var null = null;
15         var obj = {
16             prop:"yo"
17         }
18         alert(obj);
19     </    >
20 </    >
21 </    >
```

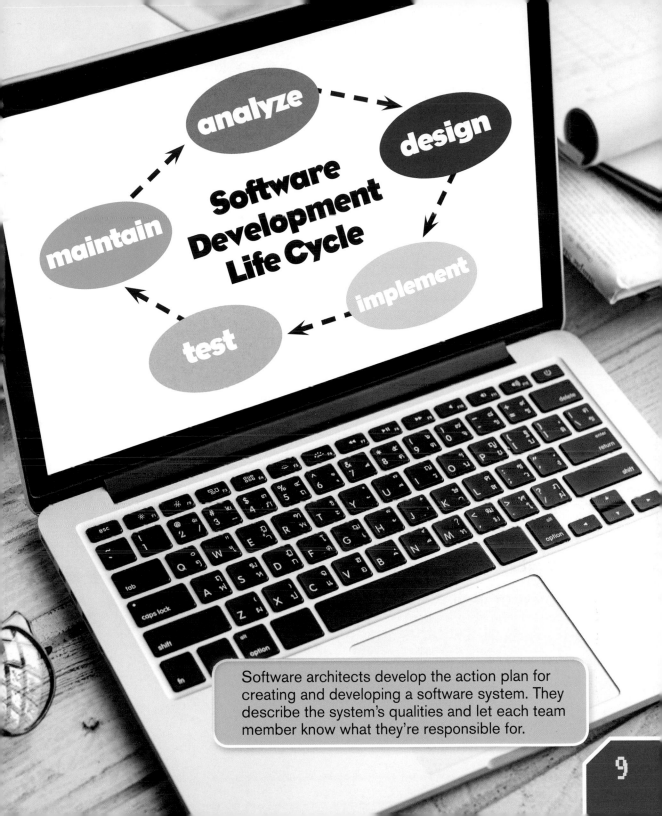

Software architects develop the action plan for creating and developing a software system. They describe the system's qualities and let each team member know what they're responsible for.

So You Want to Be an SA

Knowledge of math and **engineering** is necessary for a career as a software architect. If you think you may want to work with computers someday, it's a good idea to take computer science and advanced math courses in school. Software architects usually have a bachelor's degree in computer science, math, or software engineering. Most also have several years of computer programming experience.

A software architect with experience in computer programming has the ability to write code. This important skill makes it possible for an SA to help with challenges that programmers might face while working on a project. It also makes them more trustworthy in the eyes of the other team members, which is important in any team project.

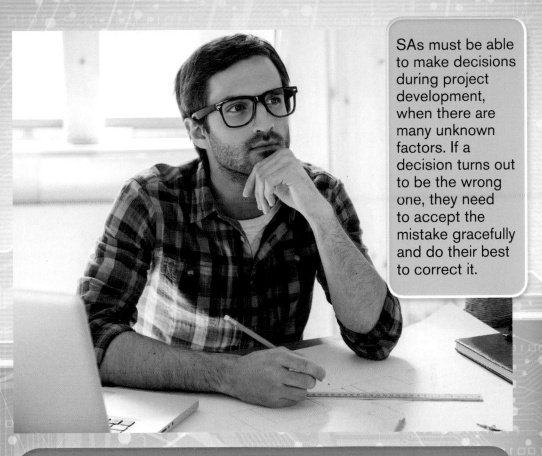

SAs must be able to make decisions during project development, when there are many unknown factors. If a decision turns out to be the wrong one, they need to accept the mistake gracefully and do their best to correct it.

Other Necessary Skills

SAs need to know a lot about computer programming but there are also many other skills they need. They must know how businesses work and understand the challenges they face. For instance, an SA may have to **anticipate** changes in a client's business policy and make sure the software their team creates will work with these changes. Researching, writing, and working with a team are also valuable skills for an SA.

How Coding Works

Code tells a computer what to do. Computers understand two types of information: on and off. Computers are basically a collection of on and off switches called transistors. Anything a computer does is based on combinations of transistors in on or off positions. The 0s and 1s of binary code represent these transistors. Modern computers contain millions of transistors, so writing a program in binary would be impossible.

Programming languages let people, such as software architects, write in code that is easier to read. These languages are translated into binary code so a computer can understand them. A programming language is a set of rules about how the code should be written.

Perl is an example of a high-level language. It's called the "Swiss Army knife" of programing languages because it can do many different things.

Tech Talk ● ● ●

Programming languages can be low level or high level. Low-level languages are closer to binary, while high-level languages are less detailed and easier for programmers to use. JavaScript is a high-level language most commonly used to create web pages. There are also mid-level languages, such as C. C is often used for gaming programs with lots of graphics, or images.

Programming Languages

It's important for software architects to know different programming languages so they can help when programmers run into problems during a project. There are dozens of programming languages, and each language is useful for different things. Some are better for writing desktop programs, while others are better for creating websites.

So how does a computer program work? If you type "Good morning!" into a program, the computer doesn't know what that means. Remember, computers only understand 0s and 1s. Your message is translated into assembly language, which is a low-level language that uses symbols to stand for binary patterns. The translated message is then sent to the computer's assembler, which is a program that changes it to machine language. Machine language is then run as binary code.

If you're creating a video game, the computer will need to know how characters should move when a player moves a joystick. Good programming will ensure a character doesn't make moves that don't make sense.

15

Choosing a Language

It's the SA's responsibility to choose the programming language for a software project. They must choose a language that fits the project. If you're making an **app** for an Android smartphone, Java is the language to use. Pascal is a language that's used mostly in educational settings. Some languages, such as Python, do a little of everything.

Another thing to think about is cost. Programming languages require development tools, which are programs that support and maintain the language. These tools can be expensive. That's why an SA must have some business sense and be aware of keeping costs low. How many people know a language may also present issues. The newest language might sound great, but if the team doesn't know how to work with it, then it's probably not the best choice.

C# is the programming language used to develop Microsoft apps. It's very similar to Java.

Java

Java may be the most popular programming language used today. It was created in the early 1990s and was supposed to be used for devices such as cell phones. However, by the time Java was released in 1996, its focus was the Internet. Now it's used almost everywhere.

An SA may choose Java for a project because it's easy to use. It's often used in computer science courses, so most software programmers know it. Since it was originally designed for cell phones that exchange data over open **networks**, it's also very secure. Another great feature is that it runs on almost any computer. In fact, the creators of Java created a catchphrase for it: WORA, which stands for "write once, run anywhere!"

Java celebrated its 20th anniversary in 2015. In early 2016, it was used by 9 million developers, ran on 7 billion devices, and powered websites such as Amazon.com and Netflix.com.

```
onlyFil
py filename

item_Event            "RDH_EVENT
#find RICname and
for i,line in enumerate
    if "<Name value="
        ricName = line
        flagCheckRicname
```

JavaScript

JavaScript is a programming language used to make interactive web pages. It's an event-driven language, which means it can respond to things like mouse clicks and typing on a keyboard. JavaScript makes web pages easier to navigate by allowing programmers to add mouse rollovers, which is when images change when users drag their mouse across the screen to see what parts are "clickable." Programmers can also use JavaScript to provide pop-up screens with helpful tips.

C++

An SA may choose to use C++ for a project. C++ is one of the older programming languages still in use. It was invented in the 1980s. It works well with other programming languages, and programs written with it are generally faster than many other programs.

C++ was an improvement over the earlier programming language C because it uses object-oriented programming (OOP). C uses procedural programming, which tells the computer what to do in steps using many lines of code. With OOP, an "object" is programmed with data and functions. The programmer then creates entirely new objects by saying they're the "children" of the original object. The children inherit the original object's information. This is a great time saver because the programmer doesn't have to write the same code over and over.

Think of objects in OOP as toy bricks. They're basic blocks, but they're designed to attach to each other to make new things that perform different functions. No matter how **complex** or different those things are, they all still have the basic features of a toy brick.

Uses of C++

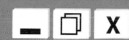

Some uses of C++ include adding high-speed graphics in video games, controlling electronic devices attached to the computer, and playing sound effects. There are some problems with using C++. While it's not quite a low-level language, it requires more code than high-level languages, which uses up more time and money. It's also difficult for new users to learn.

Other Popular Languages

New programming languages are released all the time. It's important for software architects to become familiar with as many as they can. Python is a high-level, object-oriented programming language that's becoming as popular as Java. It's easy to learn and has a built-in debugging system that increases production and reduces maintenance costs. Its language is a lot like ordinary English, so programmers don't have to learn the **syntaxes** other languages require.

Ruby is another programming language gaining popularity because it's easy to read. Ruby allows programmers to use either procedural or object-oriented programming. It's a good choice for creating websites for which programmers need to be **flexible** and deal with changing requirements. It's also a good choice if they want to experiment with new features.

The creator of Python, Guido van Rossum, wanted a name that was short, original, and mysterious for his new programming language. He was reading scripts for *Monty Python's Flying Circus*, a popular 1970s British comedy, at the same time he was creating his programming language.

The Personality of an SA

There are several important personal skills that will help an SA in their career. Most important is communication. SAs have to communicate with many different people—from programmers to clients—for each project. They shouldn't talk to clients in technical terms that might not be understood. SAs need strong leadership skills so they can support and guide their team.

The ability to analyze, or closely study, and solve problems is a must, especially with a multilevel project where many things may go wrong. Being flexible and able to deal with changes quickly is also important. An SA should be patient when dealing with the different personalities of the team members to keep them focused on a common goal.

Technology is always changing. SAs need to keep up with the latest information and learn about new programming languages, methods, and tools. To stay on top of changes in their field, SAs should take classes, attend technology conferences, and read articles written by other SAs.

Hard Work and Happiness

Harrison Ambs, lead SA at Stickboy Creative, says the best part of his job is when clients tell him how great their software is. He says he knows that work isn't usually fun, but if he can make someone's day better or easier with his software, it makes him feel good.

Related Fields

There are several other careers related to software architecture. Enterprise architects (EA) deal specifically with a client's business strategy and design a system to support it. EAs must understand their client's business so they can figure out the right technology to use for a project. An EA's main purpose is to determine where the business is now, where it should be in the future, and how technology fits in.

Application architects (AA) work with computer applications or web programs. AAs focus on designing and testing a specific program to meet the needs of a project. It's an AA's job to pay close attention to detail to make sure their program is consistent, or free from differences, and easy to maintain.

EAs may find themselves working in different types of surroundings. They might design a software system for a warehouse computer network.

Learn to Code Now!

We live in a world in which software touches many areas of our lives. Technology is becoming a greater part of our everyday activities. Coding is a skill that will be needed for almost every profession in the future. Some educators believe it's as important to learn as English or math.

Learning to code isn't just for people who want to be software architects. It also helps people develop computational thinking skills. Computational thinking is a way of solving problems by breaking them down into more manageable problems and smaller steps. These are skills everyone should have. Scientists, mathematicians, and musicians are just some of the people who can benefit from this type of thinking. It helps people understand technology of all kinds and solve problems in almost any career.

You're never too young to code. Preschool students can learn the basics of coding and computer commands before they can read! With online classes, older children can learn to create entire programs by themselves.

29

The Future of SAs

Code is the language of our digital world. The more software people and companies use, the more jobs there will be in coding fields. In 2015, the U.S. Bureau of Labor Statistics estimated that, by the year 2024, there would be more than 2 million jobs available for people in the computer system design industry.

Educators are taking note. In 2014, England changed its school curriculum to include coding courses for kids ages 5 to 15. Carnegie Mellon University in Pittsburgh, Pennsylvania, is home to the Software Engineering Institute, which offers courses and other training specific to software architects.

In 2015, *CNNMoney* rated software architect as the top job in America based on its chances of growth, pay, and work satisfaction. Software architects are creating the digital plans of our future!

Glossary

anticipate: To consider in advance.

app: A program that performs one of the major tasks for which a computer is used. "App" is short for "application."

binary code: A type of information, made up entirely of the digits 1 and 0, that is directly understood by computers when running software.

client: An individual or company that pays someone else to do something.

complex: Hard to understand.

debug: To identify software errors, which programmers call "bugs," and fix the code to correct the issues.

engineering: The study and practice of using math and science to do useful things, such as building machines.

flexible: Being able to move and bend in many ways; willing and able to change.

implement: To begin to do or use something.

network: A system of computers and databases that are all connected.

software: Programs that run on computers and perform certain functions.

syntax: How words are arranged to form a sentence.

technical: Of or relating to a mechanical or scientific subject.

technology: A method that uses science to solve problems and the tools used to solve those problems.

Index

Websites

Due to the changing nature of Internet links, PowerKids Press has developed an online list of websites related to the subject of this book. This site is updated regularly. Please use this link to access the list: www.powerkidslinks.com/bsc/sa